Personal Action Planning

How To Know What You Want and Get It

by

Dr. R. Henry Migliore
Facet Enterprises Professor of
Strategic Planning & Management
Northeastern State University/University Center at Tulsa

A Division of Harrison House Publishers
Tulsa, Oklahoma

Unless otherwise indicated, all Scripture quotations are taken from the *King James Version* of the Bible.
Other Scripture quotations are from:
— *The Amplified Bible, Old Testament* (AMP). Copyright © 1954, 1958 by The Lockman Foundation, La Habra, California.
—*The Amplified Bible, New Testament* (AMP). Copyright © 1962, 1964 by Zondervan Publishing House, Grand Rapids, Michigan.
— *The Living Bible* (TLB). Copyright © 1971 by Tyndale House Publishers, Wheaton, Illinois.
— *The Holy Bible, New International Version* (NIV). Copyright © 1973, 1978 by the International Bible Society. Used by permission of Zondervan Bible Publishers.

Personal Action Planning
How To Know What You Want and Get It
ISBN 0-89274-514-2

Managing for Success
P. O. Box 957
Jenks, Oklahoma 74037
Illustrations by Mike Kelly

Published by Honor Books
A Division of Harrison House Publishers
P. O. Box 35035
Tulsa, Oklahoma 74153

Printed in the United States of America.

On Course

The problem with life
is ....

Life is a great journey
through places and times,
but some go through it
without a map or guide!

Life is a journey.
Let the Bible be your map.
Let God be your guide,
and you shall never stray from the path.

Roscoe William Migliore
Spring 1988

Biblical Backup to Planning and Management

Commit your work to the Lord, then it will succeed.

Any enterprise is built by wise planning.

Proverbs 16:3; 24:3 TLB

May he grant you your heart's desire and fulfill all your plans.

Psalm 20:4 TLB

The Lord Almighty has sworn,

Surely, as I have planned, so it will be, and as I have purposed, so it will stand.

Isaiah 14:24,25 NIV

... What I have planned, that will I do....

Isaiah 46:11

Where there is no vision, the people perish: but he that keepeth the law, happy is he.

Proverbs 29:18

... And your young men shall see visions, and your old men shall dream dreams.

Acts 2:17

Contents

Introduction

The purpose of this book is to help people develop a long-term strategic plan for their lives. My aim is to help the reader become what the Lord intends for him to be. My hope is to stir a vision or dream and then to provide a means by which that dream may be achieved. The vision for the book came after many years of work with corporations, businesses, organizations, ministries and churches in which my primary focus was on helping them develop strategic plans and consequent methods to organize and manage. During twenty years of consulting experience with these organizations — from top Fortune 500 companies to small businesses — I also had the opportunity to help meet the needs of people seeking direction in their own lives. Always, the Bible is the main reference I have used to help people.

Five of my previously published books outline the principles and examples from organizations with which I worked during that period. They are *MBO: Blue Collar to Top Executive*, published in 1977; *An MBO Approach to Long-Range Planning*, published in 1984, *Strategic Long-Range Planning*, published in 1986 and updated in 1987, and *The Use of Strategic Planning for Churches and Ministries* and *Common Sense Management — A Biblical Perspective*, published in 1988.[1]

As I counseled with undergraduate and graduate students and people in careers up through top organization executives, I began to notice that I was, in effect, giving them the same advice I had given the organizations. I also noticed national statistics indicating that fewer than 5 percent of the people surveyed had any idea of where they wanted to be in five years. This prompted me to begin a research project of my own.

Initial Survey Results

Some of the things I have learned from the people who participated in an initial survey are:

1. 40 percent felt they had a mission or call on their lives.
2. 23 percent were not satisfied with their prospects for personal advancement on their present jobs.
3. 46 percent have a will in writing.
4. 84 percent have discussed a dream for their lives with someone close to them.
5. 46 percent feel they have done more with their lives than they thought they would.
6. 85 percent say their talents are not being used at work.
7. 84 percent say their talents are used in outside activities such as church, scouts or other groups.

Survey of Accountants

Later, in another survey of two groups of professional accountants, we found:

1. 58 percent of Group A and 53 percent of Group B did not expect to be with the same organization in five years.
2. 69 percent of A and 60 percent of B felt their talents were not being utilized on the job.
3. Both groups had 78 percent to 79 percent with measurable, five-year objectives.
4. Only 10 percent of A and 39 percent of B had a will in writing.
5. 46 percent of A participants felt a call on their lives, 36 percent of B felt a call on their lives.
6. 58 percent of A and 53 percent of B felt they wanted to be in the same jobs in five years.
7. 10 percent of A and 31 percent of B had discussed dreams and plans for their lives with their bosses.
8. 84 percent of A and 82 percent of B had discussed their dreams and plans with spouses, friends, or roommates.
9. 10 percent of A and 39 percent of B had written wills.
10. 66 percent of A and 73 percent of B had more life insurance than their companies provided.

When asked about their jobs and about available opportunities in those jobs, survey participants responded as follows:

Group A — 22 percent felt there were good

opportunities for pay/bonuses. 30 percent felt there were opportunities for recognition for well-done jobs.

Group B — 47 percent felt poor chance for pay/bonus. 53 percent felt there were chances of recognition for well-done jobs.

Survey Results of College Seniors, Graduate Students

Some salient points from a survey of college seniors and graduate students:

1. 71 percent of seniors and 59 percent of graduate students felt definite calls on their lives.
2. 85.3 percent said they came from unbroken homes, and of this group, 86 percent had definite purposes for their lives. Of the 14.7 percent who reported being from broken homes, only 56 percent felt they had purposes for their lives.
3. 87.4 percent reported discussing their dreams and plans for their lives with someone else.
4. 13 percent reported that they were not progressing as well in life as they had expected five years ago.

In a 1987 follow-up study, 62 percent of the seniors and graduate students from four different colleges believed they had a purpose in life. However, 84.5 percent had dreams of what their lives ought to be. Of the total sample, those with purpose also had objectives and discussed them with others. Generally, there were no differences between men and women respondents. Roughly two-thirds of the total sample of students felt they needed either one-year or five-year objectives. Both men and women ranked personal development and growth as a top priority goal.

Results of Other Studies

1. Of the 55 percent of marriages that end in divorce, it is estimated that 80 percent of the divorces were money related.

2. Of twelve married women today, eleven will become widows.

3. From a long-term project at the University of Minnesota came results that we all need to consider as we get to know ourselves better:[2]

A. The genetic makeup of a child is a stronger influence on personality than child rearing.

B. For most of the traits measured, more than half the variations were found to be due to heredity, leaving less than half determined by the influence of parents, home environments, and other experiences in life.

C. Among traits found most strongly determined by heredity were leadership and traditionalism, or obedience to authority.

D. Other traits that the study concluded were more than 50 percent determined by heredity included a sense of well-being and zest for life, alienation, vulnerability or resistance to stress, and fearfulness or risk-seeking.

E. The need to achieve, including ambition and an inclination to work hard toward goals, also was found to be genetically influenced, but more than half of this trait seemed determined by life experience.

If this study is valid, we can see that heredity does influence our lives. Each person should try to determine this influence on his life. We should be encouraged by the concept that we also can influence the outcome of our lives. Everything is *not* predetermined.

What does the Bible say about planning?

Proverbs 20:5 (NIV) says:

The purposes of a man's heart are deep waters.

Luke 14:28 states:

For which of you, intending to build a tower, sitteth not down first, and counteth the cost ... ?

Proverbs 24:3 says:

Through wisdom is an house builded; and by understanding it is established.

1 Corinthians 14:33 states:

For God is not the author of confusion, but of peace ....

1 Corinthians 14:40 says:

Let all things be done decently and in order.

Proverbs 16:9 (NIV) says:

In his heart a man plans his course, but the Lord determines his steps.

Armed with this information, I began to see the great need that all people have to create visions for their lives, to analyze themselves, and to set up objectives which they want to reach. That is the major focus of this book:

Where have I been? Where am I now? Where can I be if I seek the Lord's will and systematically, prayerfully, analyze how I can maximize my potential?

These principles will work at any stage of life. Grandma Moses painted her first picture at age 75, and Ray Crock was 54 when he opened his first McDonald's.

This book can be used to develop a plan for your life by following the outline. If further assistance is needed, VHS color tapes can be obtained to guide you through the book. Audio tapes are also available.

The first section of this book is designed to allow you to gain a clear picture of yourself and to get an idea of how other people look at you. You will analyze people who have had an influence on you and what these influences were. As the book progresses, each step is like a small piece of a puzzle with each part not meaning a lot until it is fitted into the whole.

Thought and care should be taken at each step. The clearer the piece of the puzzle is, the better it will fit into the overall picture. You never know what little piece, like a particular hobby or interest, might be the key to an expanded career or opportunity. Steps will be taken to determine things that make you feel good and things with which you struggle. The reader may examine the third chapter in each of my books, *An MBO Approach to Long-Range Planning* and *Strategic Long-Range Planning,* and write a one-paragraph purpose for his life. (Either of those books may be used to see how corporations develop their purpose and mission statements.) Analyzing things we like to do and do not like to do further helps us have a vision of where we can be.

Then follow the same patterns from both books and prepare an environmental analysis. This is the stage where you analyze what is going on in the world so that your plan can be based on good current information. A section is also provided for in-depth study of personal strengths and weaknesses. Luke 12:48 says:

> **For unto whomsoever much is given, of him shall be much required.**

You must analyze your strengths and utilize them. Your talents should not be wasted or misused. The planning process outlined here will help you make the most of your strengths and minimize or improve your weaknesses. By ranking goals, you can determine what is important to you on the job.

Based on the research to date, great improvement is needed in this area. Remember, in the first study mentioned, 84 percent felt their full talent was not being used on the job. A full 61 percent of one professional group said they do not want to be working for their present employer in five years. This helps you better clarify what you are looking for on the job. Because of the importance of occupation — careers or jobs — in people's lives, a major section is dedicated to helping you analyze your job and how much of your potential you are achieving on the job.

A section also is devoted to dreams and visions. The Bible explicitly admonishes us to have a dream and vision. Proverbs 29:18 says: **Where there is no vision, the people perish.** Joel 2:28 says: **Your old men shall dream dreams, your young men shall see visions.** Acts 2:17 says essentially the same thing.

After you are given an opportunity to clarify your dream and vision in writing, a very important section of this book is aimed at developing specific objectives and targets for the next five years in the following areas: spiritual, career, family, health, financial, entertainment and other areas of importance to you. The next sections are devoted to getting yourself "on the ball" and actually doing something. Closely akin to visions are expectations. The dream sets the stage, but believing and expecting are equally important. You must expect to succeed.

This book is designed to force you to think about things you must do to get started. Analyze things that are holding you back, then work on a plan to overcome these obstacles. Another important section helps you identify people who can help with your personal growth. None of us can achieve our maximum potential unassisted.

Toward the close of this book, a very workable action-planning technique I have used for years is presented. This method shows how to take a target, develop strategies, and use a step-by-step method to get into action. It concludes with developing a way of rewarding yourself and your family as you accomplish your plan. I also recommend taking some of the personality and career tests available. One of the best is *Communique*[3] which I have used in a number of businesses, churches, and ministries.

One of the most important things you ever do will be to realize that God has a purpose and a mission for your life. It is up to you to seek that call and then do everything within your power to achieve it. Most of us are not achieving our potentials and, therefore, are not becoming the servants we could be. I am praying this book will help you become the person the Lord wants you to be. Remember as you fill out the book and answer the questions there are no "right" or "wrong" answers, only facts about YOU. Also remember that each little piece of information is like a small piece of a puzzle. You cannot get a clear picture until all the pieces begin to fall into place.

Endnotes

[1] The first three books mentioned may be ordered from Managing for Success, Box 957, Jenks, Oklahoma 74037. The fourth and fifth books are available from Harrison House, P.O. Box 35035, Tulsa, Oklahoma 74153.

[2] Daniel Goleman, "Study: Nature Dominates Nurture," *The Morning Union*, Springfield, Massachusetts, November 11, 1986.

[3] For more information, contact Opliger Communications Inc., P. O. Box 781683, Wichita, Kansas 67278-1683.

Workbook

VISIONS AND DREAMS

Your Dream/Describe Yourself

Describe the vision and dream you have for your life.

How would you describe yourself to someone you have never seen?

For as he thinketh in his heart, so is he.

Proverbs 23:7

Would your friends describe you the same way? What would they say?

For by the grace given me I say to every one of you: Do not think of yourself more highly than you ought, but rather think of yourself with sober judgment, in accordance with the measure of faith God has given you.

Romans 12:3 NIV

If anyone thinks he is something when he is nothing, he deceives himself. Each one should test his own actions. Then he can take pride in himself, without comparing himself to somebody else ....

Galatians 6:3,4 NIV

List the three people who have had the greatest influence on your life.

1. ________________________________

2. ________________________________

3. ________________________________

What was the major influence from each?

1. ________________________________

2. ________________________________

3. ________________________________

List your favorite social activities and hobbies:

1. ________________________________

2. ________________________________

3. ________________________________

List three things that have made you feel good this month:

1. ________________________________

2. ________________________________

3. ________________________________

Write out a one-paragraph description of the purpose of your life.

But seek first his kingdom and his righteousness, and all these things will be given to you as well.

Matthew 6:33 NIV

Delight yourself in the Lord and he will give you the desires of your heart.

Psalm 37:4 NIV

... I urge you to live a life worthy of the calling you have received.

Ephesians 4:1 NIV

Every purpose is established by counsel.

Proverbs 20:18

- 3 THINGS YOU LIKE TO DO:

- 3 THINGS YOU DON'T LIKE TO DO:

List three things you like to do:

1. ______________________________
2. ______________________________
3. ______________________________

List three things you do not like to do:

1. ______________________________
2. ______________________________
3. ______________________________

WHAT'S GOING ON?

- WHAT ARE YOUR STRENGTHS?
- WHAT ARE YOUR WEAKNESSES?

Environmental Analysis, Strengths, and Weaknesses

What is going on in the world around you?

1. ______________________________

2. ______________________________

3. ______________________________

Commit to the Lord whatever you do, and your plans will succeed.

Proverbs 16:3 NIV

What are your major strengths?

1. ______________________________

2. ______________________________

3. ______________________________

For unto whomsoever much is given, of him shall be much required.

Luke 12:48

... Complete and proficient, well-fitted and thoroughly equipped for every good work.

2 Timothy 3:17 AMP

What are your major weaknesses?

1. ______________________________

2. ______________________________

3. ______________________________

Pride goes before destruction, a haughty spirit before a fall.

Proverbs 16:18 NIV

List some failures you have experienced in your life:

1. ______________________________
2. ______________________________
3. ______________________________

What do you see in these experiences that was less than successful?

1. ______________________________
2. ______________________________
3. ______________________________

Are these failures holding you back?

RANK YOUR JOB GOALS:

a. SATISFYING BOSS
b. STATUS
c. JOB SECURITY
d. INDEPENDENT THOUGHT
e. HIGHER SALARY
f. RECOGNITION
g. PROMOTION
h. PERSONAL GROWTH

Your Work

Rank your job goals from first to eighth:

1. ____ satisfying my boss's expectations
2. ____ prestige and status
3. ____ job security
4. ____ opportunity for independent thought and action
5. ____ higher salary, more benefits, or both
6. ____ recognition for good performance
7. ____ promotion to a better job
8. ____ personal growth and development

What do you like most about your job?

1. ______________________________
2. ______________________________
3. ______________________________

Neither do people light a lamp and put it under a bowl. Instead they put it on its stand, and it gives light to everyone in the house.

Matthew 5:15 NIV

How much of your potential do you feel you are achieving?

YOUR LIFE PLAN:

- 5 YEARS

- 1 YEAR

The Future

Write a one-paragraph description of how you want your life to be in five years.

A man's heart deviseth his way: but the Lord directeth his steps.

Proverbs 16:9

Write a one-paragraph description of how you want your life to be in one year.

OBJECTIVES:

(A) SPIRITUALLY

(B) CAREER/POSITION

(C) FAMILY

(D) HEALTH – WEIGHT, EXERCISE

(E) FINANCIAL –
INCOME, NET WORTH

(F) ENTERTAINMENT –
FUN, HOBBIES, VACATION

(G) OTHERS

HOW WILL YOU GET THERE?

Where Do You Want To Be?

In this section be specific. These are measurable objectives/goals/targets based on the foundation developed in each step from your vision up to this section.

A. Spiritually:

In five years ____________________

____

____

Next year ____________________

____

____

B. Career/Position:

In five years ____________________

____

____

Next year ____________________

____

____

C. Family:

In five years ______________________________

____

____

Next year ______________________________

____

____

D. Health/Weight, Exercise:

In five years ______________________________

____

Next year ______________________________

____

____

E. Financial/Income, Net Worth:

In five years ______________________________

____

Next year ______________________________

____

____

F. Entertainment/Fun, Hobbies, Vacation:

In five years ______________________________

____

Next year ______________________________

____

____

G. Other:

In five years ______________________________

____

____

Next year ______________________________

____

____

Put Your Plan Into Action

Commit thy works unto the Lord ....

Proverbs 16:3

A. How will you get there?

____

____

____

B. What are four things you must do in the next few months to get where you want to be next year and in five years?

1. ______________________________
2. ______________________________
3. ______________________________
4. ______________________________

C. What are four things holding you back?

1. ______________________________
2. ______________________________
3. ______________________________
4. ______________________________

- WHAT MUST YOU DO?
- WHAT'S HOLDING YOU BACK?
- OVERCOMING OBSTACLES.
- WHOSE HELP DO YOU NEED?

D. How do you overcome each of those four obstacles?

____

____

____

____

He that handleth a matter wisely shall find good....

Proverbs 16:20

E. Whose help do you need to achieve your potential and get where you want to be in five years?

1. ________________________________
2. ________________________________
3. ________________________________
4. ________________________________

Plans fail for lack of counsel, but with many advisers they succeed.

Proverbs 15:22 NIV

For lack of guidance a nation (or "a person") falls, but many advisers make victory sure.

Proverbs 11:14

WORKSHEET:

- OBJECTIVE
- STRATEGY
- ACTION PLAN

Use this worksheet to turn an objective into action.

OBJECTIVE: ______________________________

____

____

(Make it specific, measurable, and within a time frame.)

STRATEGY: ______________________________

____

____

(What are steps needed? When will you start? What will you do? Break objective down into small pieces for an action plan.)

ACTION PLAN: ______________________________

____

____

Study to shew thyself approved unto God, a workman that needeth not to be ashamed ....

2 Timothy 2:15

And whatsoever ye do in word or deed, do all in the name of the Lord Jesus ....

Colossians 3:17

I suggest copying this page and making one worksheet for each objective: spiritual, career, family, health, financial, entertainment, and any other areas you desire. Fill out each sheet, and keep them in a prominent place. Some people have taped these sheets on their refrigerator or a mirror. The key is to keep them in front of you as reminders.

- WHO CAN YOU TALK WITH?
- CAN THEY HELP YOU MONITOR?

Review and Reward

I. Review:

A. Name the person or persons with whom you can discuss your plan.

____

____

B. What will happen when you discuss your plan?

____

____

____

C. Can he or she help you monitor progress?

Yes __________ No __________

If yes ... how?

____

____

____

II. Reward yourself for accomplishment! List something specific as a reward for accomplishment of some — or all — key objectives.

____

____

____

____

____

Now he that planteth and he that watereth are one: and every man shall receive his own reward according to his own labour.

1 Corinthians 3:8

For if I do this thing willingly, I have a reward ....

1 Corinthians 9:17

... Prosperity is the reward of the righteous.

Proverbs 13:21b NIV

So then, each of us will give an account of himself to God.

Romans 14:12 NIV

When the righteous prosper, the city rejoices ....

Proverbs 11:10 NIV

Conclusion

Congratulations! Now you have completed a long-range strategic plan for your life. You are now in a select nationwide group of only 5 percent. This plan sets you apart from the crowd. Now it is time to commit this plan to intensive prayer. The Holy Spirit will give you guidance on whether or not this plan and this direction are the ones that the Lord intends for you. You will find confirmation as you proceed through the plan.

Do not think this is a completed statement. You will continually revise your plan as you move through different stages in your life. A young person starting his or her career is going to have different objectives from those of a person nearing retirement. What you have learned are the strategic planning tools and techniques. You have learned how to seek the Lord's guidance. What you will do is continually upgrade this plan as you advance through life. Carefully study the Biblical passages cited so you can better understand your life and be encouraged that there *is* a greater call for your life.

Finally, this plan can give you direction. You have taken each part of your life and fitted the pieces together. Each step in the analysis, like a piece of a puzzle, does not make sense when looking at it separately.

For example, you might ask yourself "Why analyze my weaknesses?"

The answer is that when pieced together with all the other steps, the "piece" listing your weaknesses gives you a full, complete picture of your life. Every piece of the puzzle is important — as is every step in this personal planning outline.

Once you see where you are going, you then must pursue your dreams with all the vigor and heart you can muster.

Colossians 3:23 says:

> **Whatever you do, work at it with all your heart, as working for the Lord, not for men.**

Example
(Based on my own life plan)

Purpose:

Be an educator, consultant, and writer with the goal of helping organizations and individuals fulfill their greatest potential. Be a positive Christian witness in all that I do.

Environmental Analysis:

Businesses, churches, organizations, and people need help. Only 5 percent of the people in America have a plan for their lives.

Strengths:

High energy, good education, and positive self-image.

Weaknesses:

Impatient, try to accomplish too much, a bit overweight, and high blood pressure.

Assumptions:

Interest rates will remain constant, Northeastern State University (NSU) will remain part of the University Center at Tulsa (UCAT), and I will remain in good health.

Objectives/Strategies:

Average one book and four articles a year for the next ten years. Fund our two sons' educations until year 2000. Pay off home and become a high school football and basketball coach in 1995. Buy one-half interest in Canadian fishing camp by 1990. Retire in the year 2000. Continue to be on select boards of directors. Continue to work at NSU and UCAT. Continue to attend present church.

Contingency Plan:

Son David's athletic ability will be the key factor in determining the move into coaching.

Operational Plan:

Set up my new office at UCAT by August 1, 1988, and buy an automobile with phone and dictation equipment for travel to NSU by October, 1988.

Evaluation:

Monitor progress each month. Discuss plan with all those around me. Continue to see if plan is on target.

Reward:

Either ski, hunt, fish, or find some other recreation as a reward at the end of each major project for goal accomplishment.

Appendices

Appendix A
Other Books and Articles on Careers

The justification for organizations doing career/life planning with their employees comes from the theories of psychology. The basic hypothesis is that a happy, healthy worker is a more productive one. This is pointed out in the study done on auto workers in Detroit by Arthur Kornhauser and Otto M. Reid.[1] What the employees need, in the eyes of Kornhauser and Reid, is:

> A purposeful spirit of trying to live up to their own personalities, to guide their activities in terms of future oriented self-conceptions.

In other words, the employees need help with planning their careers and lives.

In Richard Bolles' book, *What Color Is Your Parachute?*,[2] he talks about the job hunt, where to get help, where to hunt, and how to help a person begin to map his/her life strengths and weaknesses so that he/she can begin to find the career in which he/she will be the most happy. The book is written in a chatty yet informational way, and the helpful material in the back of this publication often is used by the CETA program to help young people begin to get their lives as well as their resumes together.

Self-Assessment and Career Development[3] by John P. Kotter, Victor A. Faux, and Charles C. McArthur emphasizes self-assessment. One form of assessment presented is open-ended questions: situations for reaction, reflection on past decisions, or active thinking about the person's decision-making process. Another exercise used is 24-hour diaries, and the authors recommend highly the use of the *Strong-Campbell Interest Inventory*.[4] These are combined with text on the tests and what they hope to accomplish, as well as with sources of information for job searching to help people find and land jobs that they like.

In *Career Satisfaction and Success*, the author, Bernard Huldane, outlines a system to help a person find his/her strengths and to use them. The system, called "System to Identify Motivated Skills" (SIMS), is looking for the strengths "that are used repeatedly in experiences that turned you on."[5] Throughout the book, Haldane emphasizes the knowledge of these "strengths" to maximize one's career growth potential, as well as one's own personal satisfaction with the job.

George Morrisey, in his book, *Getting Your Act Together*,[6] concentrates on setting realistic short-term goals and making practical action plans out of them. An important contribution in his concept of setting goals is to put them into "bite-sized" segments. Any discussion of this topic would be incomplete without the contributions of Ruth and Norman Vincent Peale. Dr. Peale's best-seller, *The Power of Positive Thinking*,[7] which was published thirty-four years ago, made a significant contribution to the idea that positive attitudes and a good self-image are keys to success.

In *The Bible and Business*[8] by Mark Short, Jr., the concept of the "perks" of the Christian life is introduced. Based on a study of Paul, benefits that can be expected are: love, joy, a gentle attitude, and security. I believe these "perks" are significant. If each objective outlined earlier in this book is met and the person has not achieved these benefits, then something is wrong.

The booklet, *In Times of Success*,[9] devotes one page to each of the following topics:

Be Grateful, Be Loyal, Be Humble, Keep Faithful to God, Keep Up Standards of Honesty, Keep Working Hard, Keep Giving, Be Sensitive to the Needs of Others, Keep "Things" in Perspective, Sort Out Your Aims, Keep in Touch with Reality, Keep Remembering the Past, Keep Remembering All That Money Cannot Buy, and If It All Went — What Then?

In the article, "Career Planning: Five Fatal Assumptions," Buck Blessing covers assumptions that people make about their careers. He observed that "What do I want to do?" is always asked but seldom the questions, "Why do I want to do it?" and "How do I want to do it?"[10] Also, Francis P. Martin, in *Hung by the Tongue*,[11] gives lots of career-related advice.

Luke 6:37,38 tells us that whatever we give out is multiplied back. If you criticize people, you will reap criticism. If you judge people, you will be judged. If you bless people, you will reap blessings in return. I believe all the talent in the world will not take you far if you cannot get along with the people around you.

Roger Fritz, in his book, *You're in Charge: a Guide for Business and Personal Success,*[12] provides in a very thorough way, step-by-step lists and tips on how to know yourself. His chapter on how stress effects you and your plan is helpful. A few of his tips on stress are to tell the problem to a confidant, then relax, and only then do something about the problem. Don Osgood devotes an entire book, *Pressure Points,*[13] to dealing with stress. Robert Tilton has made an important contribution to this subject with *Dare to Be a Success.*[14] This book is important because it helps a person see that he can succeed. Pastor Tilton helps us see that this is what the Lord wants for us. Dale Brown, a respected coach at LSU, has published five motivational books, and has tapes and films available. Any of Coach Brown's material will help you go into action. I also recommend *Spiritual Fitness in Business.*[15]

Endnotes

[1] Kornhauser, Arthur, and Otto M. Reid. *Mental Health of the Industrial Worker* (New York: John Wiley & Sons, Inc., 1965), p. 269.

[2] Bolles, Richard. *What Color Is Your Parachute?* (Berkeley: Ten Speed Press, 1972).

[3] Kotter, John P., Victor A. Faux, and Charles McArthur. *Self-Assessment and Career Development* (New Jersey: Edgewood Cliffs, Prentice Hall, Inc., 1978.)

[4] Ibid., p. 295.

[5] Huldane, Bernard. *Career Satisfaction and Success* (New York: AMACOM, 1974), p. 3.

[6] Morrisey, George. *Getting Your Act Together* (Santa Monica: Salenger Educational Media, 1980).

[7] Peale, Norman Vincent. *The Power of Positive Thinking* (New York: Fawcett Crest, 1952).

[8] Short, Mark Jr. *The Bible and Business* (Nashville: Broadman Press, 1978).

[9] *In Times of Success* (Zondervan Publishing, Grand Rapids, Michigan, 1979).

Other Books and Articles on Careers

[10] Blessing, Buck. "Career Planning: Five Fatal Assumptions," *Training and Development Journal,* September 1986, pp. 49-51.

[11] Martin, Francis. *Hung by the Tongue,* Lafayette, Louisiana 70909, pp. 9,10.

[12] Fritz, Roger. *You're in Charge: a Guide for Business and Personal Success* (Glenview: Scott, Foresman and Company, 1986).

[13] Osgood, Don. *Pressure Points: How to Deal With Stress* (Chappaquah: Christian Herald Books, 1980).

[14] Tilton, Robert G. *Dare to Be a Success: Achieving Your Potential* (Dallas: WOF Publications, 1986).

[15] For further information about *Spiritual Fitness in Business,* contact Probe Ministries International, 1900 Ferman Drive, Suite 100, Richardson, Texas 75081.

Appendix B
Study Results on Personal Planning

University seniors, graduate students, and professional accountants were studied to find out more about their attitudes or careers. The senior and graduate students seemed to have a more definite purpose, mission, and call in their lives than the accountants. A total of 71 percent of the seniors and 59 percent of the graduate students were very definite in concluding a particular purpose for their lives; whereas the accountants were not as definite, with 46 percent of those in CPA training and 36 percent of those in the accounting association feeling a definite call. This could be explained as the idealism of youth being tempered by the reality of the work environment.

Both students and accountants had an overall clear picture of where they wanted to be in five years. Remember the seniors and graduate students had a class assignment to develop a plan for their lives. So this would influence the 65 percent of the senior group and 78 percent of the graduate student group responding with these clear, measurable five-year objectives. However, the accountants responded with 79 percent having a clear picture of where they wanted to be in five years.

A total of 87 percent of the seniors and 95 percent of the graduate students had discussed their dreams and plans for their lives with someone close to them as compared to 83 percent of the professional accountants. When analyzing the professional accountants, it is interesting to note that more than half of the respondents did not indicate they wanted to be with the same organization in five years. Fewer than half of the professional accountants thought they had the opportunity for independent thought and action, opportunities for recognition, and opportunities for personal advancement. Again, fewer than half felt there was an opportunity for higher salary or recognition. It could be concluded that the professional accountants' skills are not being utilized on the job, and their higher-level needs are not being met on the job. This could explain why they did not expect to be with the same organization in five years. Approximately one-fourth of the professional accountants did not have life insurance over what their organization provides, with approximately one-third having a will in writing.

The purpose of this study was to gain insights into the careers of both professional accountants and the students. More extensive research is needed to verify these results. Indications, however, are that both students and accountants need to further develop visions for their lives, better refine their long-term objectives, and then follow up to implement the plans. As students will be following career paths of the professionals into a work life, evidence indicates the need to match their skills in an organization that will satisfy needs for advancement, recognition, self-esteem and personal advancement.

A later study confirmed all of the statistics of the earlier studies. In this one we asked one extra question: "Do you come from a broken home?" A total of 14.7 percent said yes. This group reported a 56 percent definite call and purpose for their lives. This statistic is shocking compared to those from traditional homes with a reported 86 percent feeling a purpose and call for their lives. This statistic helps show the devastation caused by divorce and separation.[1]

In a follow-up study in 1987, 62 percent of the seniors and MBA's from five different Western colleges believed they had a purpose in life. Of the total sample, those with purpose also had objectives and discussed them with others. Generally, there was no difference between men and women respondents. Further results in the most recent study of college students that we have just completed are:

Males and females from the colleges tested plan on a short-term basis. The majority of students (84.5 percent) always or almost always had dreams they wished to achieve in their lives. A smaller percentage (62.9 percent) indicated they always or almost always believed they had a purpose in their lives. Only 54.3 percent said they always or almost always talked over their dreams with others. This could be an indication that accountability gives confidence and motivation. Students who do believe they have a purpose in their lives generally discuss their goals with others. Those who do not believe they have a purpose in their lives do not discuss their goals. Other important results were:

1) 62.2 percent plan their use of time on a daily basis (women 66.9 percent, men 58.4 percent); 2) 63.6 percent plan on a weekly basis; 3) only 3.8 percent do not plan their use of time; 4) 8.5 percent said they seldom or never felt they had a purpose for their lives, but 84.5 percent believed they always or almost always do; 5) about two-thirds felt they needed one-year objectives; 6) only about two-thirds believed they needed five-year objectives; 7) 75.2 percent of all students believed they needed measurable objectives; 8) both male and female groups ranked personal growth and development as the most important job goal (personal growth and development being ranked significantly more important by females); and 9) overall, prestige and status ranked least important (males placed prestige and status higher on the scale — seventh — than did the females — ranked eighth).

One Western school had a significant difference with women believing they had purpose more than the men (women — 69.2 percent, men — 39.4 percent). Daily planning from this same school ranked women at 76.9 percent, and men 48.5 percent. We are looking into that one school to see why the difference in women versus men.

Endnote

[1] Many sections of the personal planning study were accomplished while working with John Iida and Cindy Mercer. Their Oral Roberts University Master's Thesis covers the material in this appendix in greater detail.

Appendix C
Comments From Others

"I'm excited! Although the seminar on Saturday hurt in some ways, it always hurts to have to change, and it was really needed in my life. Thanks for the opportunity to attend."

"This is just a short note to say thanks for your *Personal Planning Seminar* that I attended. The concepts you shared in the seminar were not new to me, but I finally heard them presented in a way that I could understand and apply. I am extremely thankful for the opportunity to attend a seminar like this and would highly recommend it to anyone wishing to make progress in their personal life. Thanks again!"

"I attended your seminar last weekend and I believe it is changing my life. Saturday evening, my wife and I sat down and started the preliminary strategic plan, and it really set her free also. She said she never realized the deep-seated resentment she harbored toward my handling of the finances."

"The material presented is practically applicable to life, Word based, and covers significant issues."

"It really made me realize how important money is — and the *wisdom* that is required in dealing with it."

"It makes you think about your future! How to plan for your future."

"It deals with the practical things of life that are usually not covered in other courses. Good, practical, real life information!"

"I enjoyed every single class. It was all very interesting — things that I plan on using in the future."

"The course is very practical and very interesting."

"... applying the Word of God to financial management, including savings."

"I was motivated to think about my life."

"The knowledge received was on practical life information."

"It helped me to realize the importance of goal setting, of being organized, and of planning for the future."

Appendix D*

Date	Jan	Feb	Mar	Apr	May	Jun	Jul	Aug	Sep	Oct	Nov	Dec
Housing												
Food												
Entertainment												
Utilities												
Phone												
Clothing												
Cleaners												
Haircut												
Medical												
Gasoline												
Car Tag												
Car Insurance												
Health Insurance												
Life Insurance												
Gifts												
Taxes												
Household												
Miscellaneous												
Church												
Allowance												
TOTAL COSTS												
INCOME												
TOTAL INCOME												
DIFFERENCE												
CUMULATIVE DIFFERENCE												

* Worksheet developed by Rinne Martin, associate professor in the Oral Roberts University School of Business.

Readings

Planning Your Life To Be a Winner: The Margin Is Jesus

1. The difference between the winner of the PGA Golf Tournament and the tenth player is an average of one stroke, the fiftieth player only four strokes. You have to be a really good golfer to even be in the top 200, but a margin of only six strokes separates the top from the 200th player.

2. In a study of aerodynamics, one learns that the leading portion of the wing provides most of an airplane's lift. Of all the square feet of space in the plane, only this very small area up and down each wing provides the margin to lift the plane.

3. The launching of the Columbia spaceship was an intricate maneuver. Everything had to be exact in terms of the centrifugal force of the earth's movement, the launching speed, and the power as the spaceship was thrust into space. The slightest margin of error on the launch would have caused the spaceship to be off hundreds of thousands of miles as it went into orbit.

4. Everyone enjoyed the NCAA basketball championship playoff a few years ago between Georgetown and North Carolina. They played shot-for-shot and point-for-point for forty minutes. With fifteen seconds to go and Georgetown

behind by one point, the final play of the game was the margin of difference between being the NCAA champion and finishing in second place.

5. If you study a football game, you will find that five or six key plays make the difference in the game. If the coaches knew which plays these would be, they would practice all week on those particular plays to be sure they are executed with perfection. The problem is that out of the eighty to one hundred plays executed, one does not know which are the key plays. This forces players to execute with precision on all of the plays so that the six or seven are executed properly. The margin for winning boils down to a very few plays.
6. The difference between winning and losing in our lives can be measured by the margin. Whenever the marginal play comes along, you will excel, and in the process, become all that you can be.
7. As much as we want to think of something as glamorous and fascinating, there is always a gritty side we have not seen. The most precious gem was once buried in dirt — and to be truly beautiful — it must be polished and cut and set in the right light. In its original state it was just as worthy, but its full potential was not known until someone recognized it and was willing and patient enough to set it free. The right amount of polishing is needed so you can realize your potential. It is not necessarily what we see on the outside that makes anyone or anything beauty. It is that glow from the inside. There is always work to be done, a need to keep on refining, polishing, and simplifying. Every person has the opportuni-

ty to receive that inner glow, to be refined and polished. All we have to do is accept Jesus as our personal Savior. He provides the margin we need as we make our walk through life.

8. We owe it to ourselves to bring out the best of who we are — to use our talents for something beautiful — and worthy. That requires a staying power that comes only with vision and determination.

9. You need a plan to become what the Lord wants you to be. Here are the essential steps: a) have a vision/dream, b) get the facts, be aware of what is going on around you, c) analyze your strengths and weaknesses, d) make a few assumptions, e) set definite measurable objectives, f) be in a state of continual prayer (God will confirm, through the Holy Spirit, what is right for you), g) develop a list of strategies for each objective, h) put the plan into action, i) review progress, and j) reward yourself for accomplishment.

"Point of View"
Work: It Isn't All That Bad

Most of us, for a period of forty years or more, spend about a third of our time working. By this, we mean at some gainful occupation to earn a living or to contribute to family income. Or it may be at home-making, although full-time homemakers are becoming fewer and fewer as wives swell the work force.

Work is something that is taken for granted. Even the Bible encourages man to be work-oriented. Genesis (9:7 and 1:28) emphasizes that it is not each man's *right* to work, but instead, it is his *duty*. Time, of which work takes a major part, is a gift from God, not to be misused.

With this as a major premise, let us explore some views about working.

As Shakespeare observed, we all pass through different stages in our lives. In each stage, the work ethic takes on a different perspective to us.

The teenage youngster takes a dim view of work. In an earlier day, the teenager's contribution was critical to the well-being of the rural American family. Large families were needed to survive in those rugged days.

In today's more affluent society, and with family work not available, the young people do not contribute to the family's economic well-being. However, if the teenager does not have responsibilities to accomplish, he loses the opportunity to learn to be accountable.

Work has evolved into more of a process of learning, discipline, and pride.

As we move into high school and college, work represents an opportunity to earn the means of acquiring what we perceive to be indispensable needs: our first car, record albums, and extras that Dad will not or cannot pay for.

When we set out on our careers, work becomes an extension of ourselves. Success on the job seems to relate to our success as a person. For some reason, one's worth to society seems based on one's job. This perception, in my opinion, does not hold in the Lord's eye. I believe He has a purpose for each of us, and each contribution is needed in all fields and at all levels.

At some point, after we have become somewhat accomplished as an electrician, tool and die maker, college professor, or electrical engineer, we become recognized for our craftsmanship and abilities. Here the work ethic takes on a whole new meaning. Work can become engrossing and something in which we take pride.

During these years, it is vital not to let work become so all-consuming that it distorts our perspective about other aspects of life. Too many people are successful in their careers, but strike out as husbands, wives, fathers, or friends. We must work — but work should not become a devouring monster.

Finally, we phase out of the work force and enter retirement — what we have looked forward to as the harvest years: leisure, travel, golf, fishing. But, all too often, disillusionment rears its ugly head. Instead of fulfillment, a sense of deprivation assails us when we are taken from our work. As retirement age gets lower and lower, more and more of us become susceptible to this problem.

If you hold the view that work is not necessary to our happiness, consider the plight of someone who suddenly becomes unemployed. It is a traumatic, insecure, frightening time. If you are not sure how much you care about your job today, consider how you would feel if you did not have it tomorrow.

The whole point of these musings is to emphasize the importance of work, to better understand the concept of working, and to show that work is as important in God's eyes as attending church on Sunday and the various other privileges we take for granted.

If we spend half of our waking hours at work, does it not make sense to put ourselves more wholeheartedly into it? If that much of our waking time is going into that particular activity, our efforts should be the very best we can put forth. Work should be taken as a natural, normal, healthful function, and as an opportunity to achieve.

Would that we all could have Pete Rose's spirit. In discussing the modern National League record he set by hitting in thirty-eight straight games — a streak which he later extended to forty-four games — and his career in baseball, he said on nationwide television:

"I love to play baseball; I can't believe I'm paid to do it."

Work might go better for us if we shared this attitude.

[Reprinted by permission of *The Tulsa Tribune*, 318 South Main Street, Tulsa, Oklahoma, from the September 18, 1978, issue, p. 11 C.]

"Point of View" Threads Influencing Our Lives

As we all journey through life, we inevitably cross the paths of those who seem to have a positive influence on our lives. In my own life, there were teachers, coaches, relatives, friends in the church, and others who had a positive influence on me.

After a recent fishing trip to Mexico for the famed Lake Guerrero large-mouth bass, I began to see how the concept of "the thread of influence" and bass fishing share something in common. We are hooked early in life by positive-influence factors, and a thread follows us all the days of our lives tying us back to those influences.

In many ways, I was like the Guerrero bass on my first leave from basic military service in the summer of 1957. Like the big bass, I had wanted my freedom and had joined the military service on my 17th birthday. I had come from a wonderful Christian home with all the love and care that could possibly be lavished on a young, energetic, often unruly, sports-minded teenager. No matter how hard I tried to shake the hook, that thread of influence remained there.

When we were going into the city for our first leave, members of my squadron poured into a tattoo parlor calling me names because I would not follow. As thin as that line of influence was, I could not go in because of the thought of later having to face my parents.

This is not to say there is anything inherently wrong about being tattooed, but it was not right for me. My parents had planted seeds of influence so that as I made decisions a thousand miles from home, their influence of right or wrong was still there.

As I have progressed through life, many, many times the often thin, fragile thread of influence from another person's life has directed me through the temptations and trials that we face as human beings. This concept of the thread of influence should encourage us all to hook as many around us as we can with loving, positive contributions to their lives so that they will be inescapably tied as they live out their lives.

At this stage, each of our children is a real blessing. For better or worse, they are energetic, independent, and excited about life. Like their father, they have an independent streak. But there is a thread tied to each of their lives, and it will follow them all of their days. It *can* be a comforting, supporting influence.

The concept is obvious. Those positive, loving, stroking, guiding influences are there, and you cannot get loose even if you try. All of us need to examine and acknowledge the threads tied to us by others. Thank God for them and be grateful. Then go about the business of tying good, positive threads.

(*The Tulsa Tribune*, April 2, 1984, reprinted by permission.)

"Point of View" The Difference Between Success and Failure

The difference between success and failure is very small ....[1]

God's Word tells us what makes the difference between success and failure in our lives:

If you want favor with both God and man, and a reputation for good judgment and common sense, then trust the Lord completely; don't ever trust yourself.

> **In everything you do, put God first, and he will direct you and crown your efforts with success.**
>
> **Proverbs 3:5,6 TLB**

---

[1] See "Planning Your Life To Be a Winner: The Margin Is Jesus."
[Reprinted from *Through the Bible* in '82, October 21.]

"Point of View" Care, Feeding of a Boss

Each of us, beginning literally with birth, develops a continuing series of relationships with other people. Without realizing it, we develop relationships with parents, siblings, and other relatives.

As we grow older, we learn to deal with teachers, counselors, scoutmasters, athletic coaches, and pastors.

Later comes college, and some of us even become skilled in the gamesmanship between ourselves and the faculty. Some of us have even had the rare opportunity to get to know a drill sergeant in the military.

Eventually, most of us — for which society is grateful — go to work and begin paying taxes. That is when we cease to live off the system and become a contributing part. That is when the game of life takes some dramatic changes. At that point, we develop a brand-new and most vital relationship — that with our new bosses.

This new boss is a person, too, and he has gone through the same stages that we have. The difference, and it is a big difference, is that he is one step ahead of us. He has power: the ability to reward and punish, both openly and subtly.

Because of this, we tend to assume that this formidable person has the keen insight to manage us properly. Some of us fail to realize that while we are learning how to deal with him, he also has a boss to contend with along with all of the problems associated with that relationship.

As I have operated in management positions through a wide range of positions in industry and academia, and consulted and advised in a wide range of organizations, I have had the opportunity to study this process, both as player and as an onlooker.

I have noted that the state of uncertainty of all players in the game as to where they stand in the organization is a common denominator that threads through this entire process. This is accompanied by a fair degree of anxiety and apprehension as to what is expected of one by higher management levels and whether one is meeting those expectations.

I believe it is important to recognize this as a natural process and that steps should be taken to cope. If these steps relieve the uncertainty, performance might be improved. As starters, I propose the following steps:

1. Ask your boss to develop a list of five key, specific, measurable results he wants you to accomplish over the next year.

2. Simultaneously, develop a similar list for yourself — what you believe you should accomplish during the next year.

3. Meet and discuss your lists. Be prepared for some disagreement between them.

4. Reach agreement on what you are to accomplish. Knowing what is expected of you will give you direction and thus increase your sense of security.

5. Now get with it, making sure that you manage your resources well to assure the results.

6. Keep your boss informed on your progress. He does not like surprises.

7. At year end, review the year, see where you stand, and then start the process over again.

What most employees fail to understand is that their primary responsibility is to make sure their boss is successful, to help prevent his making a mistake. You can be sure that your boss wants to be successful. He has you on the team to help ensure that success. If he has any reason to suspect you of disloyalty or of failure to work for the common good, you are in trouble.

The seven steps listed above help you assure the boss that you are on target with his expectations.

It is also important to recognize that his perception of your contribution is of prime importance — and not necessarily your own perception. With this in mind, is it not a good idea to find out from him exactly what results he expects?

As you study ways and means to "care for and feed your boss," be sure that you honor and respect the responsibility he has. Make sure you are loyal to the cause and are making a contribution.

[Reprinted by permission of *The Tulsa Tribune,* from its March 17, 1978, issue, p. 15 F.]

"Point of View"
Employee Care, Feeding

A few weeks ago in this column, I discussed the care and feeding of the boss. I pointed out the importance of his relationship, how it should be nurtured, and how to aggressively seem to keep it in good repair and in a healthy state. I suggested that one should develop a set of accountable objectives and results one hoped to achieve during a given time period, discuss these with the boss, and keep him posted on one's progress. Such a step would provide a firm fix on a goal and on achieving it.

In today's discussion, we change perspective. We turn our attention the other way and discuss the care and feeding of those who work for us, or those under our direction for supervision. What provides the most important job satisfaction to them? What motivates them the most effectively?

In surveys of dozens of large and small businesses, corporations, banks, and nonprofit organizations, I have learned that achievement and recognition are paramount goals of a wide cross-section of people ranging from welders and bank tellers to upper management. That gives us our first focal point on care and feeding of our employees. As Charles Kothe, the law school dean at Oral Roberts University, often says in his lectures:

"These higher-level needs are as important in our business as blood and air are to the physical body."

Our first step, then, as managers of people is to make sure we recognize these needs and properly feed the souls of those who work for us. Think of all the people who report to you.

Ask yourself, "When was the last time I provided each of them with some means of positive recognition?"

This might range from a pat on the back and a warm "thank you" to a notation on a piece of business correspondence that was well-handled or some type of comment in front of a group. If you cannot remember the last time, I suggest that you are derelict and that you should begin to look for some accomplishments to recognize.

After that, you might ask each employee to spell out to you what he hopes to accomplish over another time frame. Consider your own expectations and make an agreement. Make sure this is a review process. What better time than this to hand out good, positive reinforcements and to analytically discuss points that have failed to measure up to your expectations?

Caution: You are analyzing performance, not the person. We all tend to safeguard and preserve our self-image, therefore we respond quickly to an attack on it — real or imagined. If you erred in equating performance with the soul of the person, you have really "pulled a boner." So keep your focus on performance. When reviewing performance, let the employee present his evaluation first. He will likely be more candid and less defensive if he has first say. This makes your own evaluation easier when your turn comes. You must be genuinely interested and able to project this interest when you talk with your employees. Unless you have their firm support, you are on shaky ground. It is their job to make you successful, and your job is to help them develop to their potential as individuals.

Be sure you never take credit for others' deeds or ideas. If you take someone's name off a report, for instance, and substitute your own and submit it to your boss, thus receiving the credit, you can be certain the person working for you who really did the work will resent the deceit and will not be disposed kindly toward you in the future. You are that person's only key voice to the next higher level of management. Be sure that you properly represent his interest.

Your name is probably well-known in each of your employees' homes. Because you are the boss and wield a fair amount of formal and informal power, the employee is ever conscious of your management style. If you doubt this, notice at the next company picnic, banquet, or outing, that the employees' families immediately recognize your name.

Many managers are unaware of the important role they play in the psychological well-being of the employee. The employee can shout at his wife, whip the kids, kick the dog, and shake his finger at the news commentator, or government officials. But he is denied using these tactics on you, the boss. He is limited to subtle signals that are sometimes almost unconsciously given. I suggest that you learn to tune in on these signals if you want to know how your people feel. Their proper care and feeding depends on how well you listen and provide the proper nourishment where the hunger is the greatest: self-esteem, achievement, and a feeling of worth.

[Reprinted by permission of *The Tulsa Tribune.*]

"Point of View"
A Look Toward the Year 2000

It is easier to predict that changes of great magnitude will take place from 1985 to the year 2000 than it is to pinpoint when those changes and specific events will take place. A futurist can always say there will be upheavals, highs and lows, political instability, wars and rumors of wars. That is relatively easy because it reflects man and how he has conducted his affairs through the centuries.

But in 1960, few of us would have been able to predict specifically what was going to happen during the years up through 1975. In 1960, would any of us have predicted a presidential assassination, the removal of a president of the United States from office, the rise of the Organization of Petroleum Exporting Countries (OPEC), and staggering inflation? The answer in most cases is no. We knew things were going to change dramatically. We just did not know what the changes would be and when they would take place.

A review of the economic literature shows that in the short term — over the next few years — all sources tend to hover near center stage. Few predict anything dramatic in the way of inflation, interest rates, job shifts, and business activity. If you extended that thought, predictions made only for the next few years would *always* stay near the center line. And when extended, they would show nothing dramatic happening by the year 2000. That is an inherent weakness in short-term forecasting.

We know that something unpredictable and dramatic is going to take place by the year 1990. So, if nothing else, we must prepare ourselves for handling a dramatic change. The only way I know of to be prepared is to have a very sophisticated long-range planning process in place.

The time and expense of preparing long-range plans will have a payoff when major events take place, and an organization leader can bring in his experienced team. They will be able to fine-tune and make orderly changes within a decision framework. The people who will be in trouble are those who manage by "the seat of their pants," who have no idea of where they are or where they are going. When they make the decision that will likely make or break their organizations, they will be taking a shot in the dark.

How do we predict where major events are to happen before the year 2000? The best way to start is to look at basic underlying factors. In the United States, we have rapidly become a service economy. As we lose steelmaking, shipbuilding, and other basic industries, we are setting the stage for an OPEC repeat. Someone is going to take advantage of our weakness and put us in exactly the same position OPEC did in the '70s.

The second area is to look for political uncertainty. There are any number of hot spots, including

South Africa, that could create a chain effect that will ripple through to the year 2000.

The third area is economic. You can look at any Economics 101 freshman course and see that there are a series of cycles in economic behavior. Over the next fifteen years, you can count on a major high and a major low. Again, no one can predict when either will happen.

The highs will follow the same pattern as the oil-drilling industry, and the bottom will just fall out with few people seeing the red flags signaling that the change is coming. The key again is the strategic planning system that gets the organization adapting quickly during the upturn and adapting even faster for the downturn.

Peter Drucker, in his article, "The Shape of Industry to Come," contends that demographic and technological change will be the factors having the greatest effect on the future shape of our nation.

If you want to peer into the future and take a look at the year 2000, watch the shape of demographic and technological changes. Count on a few major changes that you will not be able to predict. Have a mindset to be able to cope and react, and it will be an interesting time at the turn of the century. You will not have a really clear picture of the year 2000, but you will be able to see a fuzzy image.

[Reprinted by permission of *The Tulsa Tribune,* from its November 6, 1985, issue.]

"Point of View"
Predicting the Unpredictable

If you read a "Point of View" column which I wrote last November, "A Look Toward the Year 2000," you noted that I predicted three major occurrences by the year 2000. This was based on the fact that it is easier to predict that changes of great magnitude will take place than it is to pinpoint *when* those changes will take place.

A futurist can always say there will be upheavals, highs and lows, political instability, wars and rumors of wars. That is relatively easy because it reflects man and how he has conducted his affairs through the centuries. The predictions were:

1. We know that something unpredictable and dramatic is going to take place by the year 1990.

2. Look for political uncertainty. There are any number of hot spots, including South Africa, that will create a chain effect that will ripple through to the year 2000.

3. Over the next fifteen years, you can count on a major economic high and a major low. Again, no one can predict when either will happen.

I then concluded that all of us must be ready to cope and react to a quickly changing world.

The day that column was published, who would have predicted a space shuttle disaster, an air attack on Libya, or a nuclear disaster in the Soviet Union? To me, these events are *prima facie* evidence that we can count on more of the same.

Let's look at those three predictions and speculate further:

1. Maybe the three events mentioned were predictable now that we examine facts surrounding their occurrence. Something even more unpredictable is coming.

2. Add Libya to the original list and be ready.

3. We are searching for the economic high. Anyone who doubts that "what goes up must come down" needs only to refresh his memory with the prices of oil, gold, and silver.

In conclusion, don't panic. Look at the horizon. Do not get caught napping. Look at the great opportunities. Adapt when the world changes and do more than just survive in this ever-changing world. Live life to the fullest.

[Reprinted by permission of *The Tulsa Tribune* from its May 9, 1986, issue.]

"Point of View"
Twenty Sure Ways To Lose Money

After twenty years of helping people solve business and personal problems, I have discovered a few ways to lose one's hard-earned money. Listen carefully for these phrases, and your objective will soon be attained:

— This opportunity is available for only a short time ....

— You have been selected as a winner of a fabulous prize. You must ....

— All your friends are in on this ....

— You have earned the right, through your success, to be considered for ....

— I am a (Christian, member of a lodge or club, and so forth). Do business with me ....

Keep talking to the person who has this opening line and soon he will have, as the popular country song says, "the gold mine, and you will have the shaft."

Here are some rules to consider if your aim is to lose your money quickly:

1. Let someone else, preferably someone you do

not know, bring you the investment idea. If they come to your door, by all means, let them in.

2. Constantly worry and plot against paying taxes. Find ways to lose so that you can deduct the losses from your taxes.

3. Be a recognized professional with your name in the yellow pages, such as a doctor or a dentist.

4. Be arrogant and have a "godlike" air.

5. Try to get rich quickly.

6. For the ultimate experience, invest money you cannot afford to lose.

7. Respond quickly with action when your mate says, "Why don't you do as well as _________?"

8. Give your mate and children credit cards and no budget.

9. Send your children to college with no accountability. Provide a car, if possible. Keep them in college no matter what.

10. Use the phone and save those letters, postcards, and stamps.

11. Buy raw land, the farther away from home, the better.

12. Build your wife a bigger closet.

13. Go into a business you know nothing about.

14. Do not develop a personal life plan, a financial plan, or set goals.

15. Do not buy insurance of any kind.

16. Do not make out your own personal will. Watch your loved ones from Heaven while they fight over your estate and give most of it to lawyers.

17. Get a divorce.

18. Do a lot of impulse buying.

19. Keep all your money for yourself. Do not give to your church or any worthy cause.

20. Do not ask for any advice from professionals in banking, insurance, law, investments, and accounting.

This column is meant to make all of us think before we spend. We all have most likely made some poor economic decisions and learned good lessons. Our quality of life can be affected by our economic decisions. It is to be hoped that we will be more careful and think through how we invest and spend our money.

[Reprinted by permission of *The Tulsa Tribune* from its August 21, 1987, issue.]

Biblical Outline of Planning Process

Purpose, Mission, Vision

Proverbs 11:14:

> "For lack of guidance a nation [or in our case 'a person'] falls, but many advisers make victory sure." (NIV)

Proverbs 15:22:

> "Plans fail for lack of counsel, but with many advisers they succeed." (NIV)

Proverbs 20:18:

> "Every purpose is established by counsel ...."

Proverbs 16:20:

> "He that handleth a matter wisely shall find good ...."

Proverbs 29:18:

> "Where there is no vision, the people perish ...."

Proverbs 23:7:

> "As a man thinketh in his heart, so is he" (paraphrased).

Joel 2:28:

> "... Your old men shall dream dreams, your young men shall see visions."

Acts 2:17:

(Essentially the same as Joel 2:28.)

Romans 12:3:

"For by the grace given me I say to every one of you: Do not think of yourself more highly than you ought, but rather think of yourself with sober judgment, in accordance with the measure of faith God has given you." (NIV)

Galatians 6:3,4:

"If anyone thinks he is something when he is nothing, he deceives himself. Each one should test his own actions. Then he can take pride in himself, without comparing himself to somebody else ...." (NIV)

Ephesians 4:1:

"... I urge you to live a life worthy of the calling you have received." (NIV)

Psalm 37:4:

"Delight yourself in the Lord and he will give you the desires of your heart." (NIV)

Matthew 6:33:

"But seek first his kingdom and his righteousness, and all these things will be given to you as well." (NIV)

Environmental Analysis

Proverbs 25:2:

"It is the glory of God to conceal a thing: but the honour of kings is to search out a matter."

Strengths and Weaknesses

Luke 12:48:

"To whom much is given, much is required" (paraphrased).

2 Timothy 3:17:

"... Complete and proficient, well-fitted and thoroughly equipped for every good work." (AMP)

Objectives

Nehemiah 2:4:

"For what dost thou make request? ..." (What do you want?)

Strategy

Matthew 5:15:

"Neither do people light a lamp and put it under a bowl. Instead they put it on its stand, and it gives light to everyone in the house" (paraphrased).

Operational Plan

2 Timothy 2:15:

"Study to shew thyself approved unto God, a workman that needeth not to be ashamed ...."

2 Timothy 3:17:

"... Complete and proficient, well-fitted and thoroughly equipped for every good work." (AMP)

Luke 14:28:

"For which one of you when he wants to build

a tower does not sit down and calculate the cost?" (paraphrased).

James 1:23:
"For if any be a hearer of the word, and not a doer, he is like unto a man beholding his natural face in a glass."

1 Corinthians 14:40:
"Let all things be done decently and in order."

1 Corinthians 16:9:
"For a great door and effectual is opened unto me, and there are many adversaries."

Philippians 4:13:
"I can do all things through Christ which strengtheneth me."

Colossians 3:17:
"And whatsoever ye do in word or deed, do all in the name of the Lord Jesus ...."

Proverbs 16:9:
"We should make plans — counting on God to direct us." (TLB)

Proverbs 16:3:
"Commit thy works unto the Lord ...."

Colossians 3:23:
"Whatever you do, work at it with all your heart, as working for the Lord, not for men ...." (NIV)

Nehemiah 2:4:
"... For what dost thou make request? So I prayed to the God of heaven."

Plan in General

Proverbs 15:22:

"Plans fail for lack of counsel, but with many advisers they succeed." (NIV)

Proverbs 16:10:

"A divine sentence is in the lips of the king: his mouth transgresseth not in judgment."

Proverbs 19:20:

"Hear counsel and receive instruction, that thou mayest be wise …."

Proverbs 20:5:

"A plan in the heart of a man is like deep water" (paraphrased).

Proverbs 24:3:

"Through wisdom is an house builded; and by understanding it is established."

Reward

1 Corinthians 3:8:

"Now he who plants and he who waters are one; but each will receive his own reward according to his own labor" (paraphrased).

Proverbs 13:21:

"… The righteous will be rewarded with prosperity" (paraphrased).

Philippians 3:14:

"I press toward the mark for the prize of the high calling of God in Christ Jesus."

Syllabus for Video Tapes

SECTION A

"Develop a Plan for Your Life"

Assignment: Fill out each step of the planning process in the personal planning book.

UNIT I

1. Develop a personal plan for your life.
2. What does the Bible say in support of a life plan?
3. Who were the people that influenced your life?

Text: *Personal Action Planning: How To Know What You Want and Get It*

UNIT II

1. What are your favorite activities and hobbies?
2. List three things that made you feel good this month.
3. Write a one-paragraph description of the purpose of your life.
4. What is the definition of the word *foundation?*
5. List three things you like to do.
6. List three things you don't like to do.

7. What is going on in the world around you?
8. List your strengths.
9. List your weaknesses.

Text: *Personal Action Planning: How To Know What You Want and Get It*

UNIT III

1. Rank your job goals.
2. What were the three top ranked goals?
3. What do you like most about your job?
4. What needs improvement in your job?
5. What problems are people having?
   Responses to questions.

Text: *Personal Action Planning: How To Know What You Want and Get It*

UNIT IV

1. What does the Bible say about visions and dreams?
2. Write a one-paragraph description of how you want your life to be in five years.
3. Write a paragraph for the first year.
4. List objectives for your spiritual life.
5. List objectives for your career.
6. List objectives for your family.
7. List objectives for your health.
8. List objectives for your financial situation.

9. List objectives for entertainment.

Text: *Personal Action Planning: How To Know What You Want and Get It*

UNIT V

1. What are the criteria for objectives?
2. What problems are people having? Responses to questions.
3. How to solve problems through interaction.
4. How to control money in a non-profit setting.

Text: *Personal Action Planning: How To Know What You Want and Get It*

UNIT VI

1. What is the major obstacle in your life?
2. List the things you need to do this month to actualize your plan.
3. What are five obstacles holding you back?
4. List the people whose help you need to reach your objectives?

Text: *Personal Action Planning: How To Know What You Want and Get It*

UNIT VII

1. How to keep your plan on target.
2. How to avoid the New Year's Eve syndrome.
3. How to develop an action plan.

4. How do you control the plan?
5. Methods of sharing your plan with someone else.
6. Ways to use a reward system.
7. Topics covered:

   Foundation

   Strengths and Weaknesses

   Where Do I Want To Be in the Future

   Work Backwards ... Where To Go Next?

   Identify Obstacles

   Document on Paper

   Control: Check Each Thing Off

   Reward System

Text: *Personal Action Planning: How To Know What You Want and Get It*

Now transfer the plan for your life into a typed version. If possible, put it on a word processor so it can be updated easily.

A one-hour review version of the entire process outlined in this book — as well as more information on either version — is available from:

Managing for Success
P. O. Box 957
Jenks, Oklahoma 74037

R. Henry Migliore of Jenks, Oklahoma, is Facet Enterprises Professor of Strategic Planning and Management, Northeastern State University/ University Center at Tulsa. Dr. Migliore teaches at the graduate and undergraduate levels. He served as professor of management and as dean of the ORU School of Business from 1975 until 1987.

He is a former manager of the press manufacturing operations of Continental Can Company's Stockyard Plant. Prior to that, he was responsible for the industrial engineering function at Continental's Indiana plant. In this capacity, Dr. Migliore was responsible for coordinating the long-range planning process. In addition, he has had various consulting experiences with Fred Rudge & Associates in New York and has served large and small businesses, associations and nonprofit organizations in various capacities.

He has made presentations to a wide variety of clubs, groups, and professional associations.

Dr. Migliore has been selected to be on the faculty for the International Conferences on Management by Objectives and the Strategic Planning Institute Seminar Series. He is also a frequent contributor to the Academy of Management, including the presentation of a paper at the 50th anniversary national conference.

He was included in a recent list of top-31 scholars, consultants, and writers in America.

He is on the Board of Directors of T. D. Williamson, Inc., the American Red Cross/Tulsa Chapter, and was previously on the board of the International MBO Institute, and Brush Creek Ranch. He also is chairman of a scholarship fund for Eastern State College. In 1984, he was elected into the Eastern State College Athletic Hall of Fame. Dr. Migliore has been a guest lecturer on a number of college campuses. He serves on four Chamber/Civic Committees, and is on the Administrative Board at The First United Methodist Church, Tulsa.

To date previous articles on management and business subjects have appeared in *AII E Journal, Construction News, Management World, Management of Personnel Quarterly, Journal of Long-Range Planning, Dental Economics, Health Care Management Review, MBO Journal, Business and Society Review, Parks and Recreation Journal, The Journal of Business Strategy, Daily Blessing, Ozark Mountaineer, On Line, Real Estate Today,* and the *Planning Review.*

His books — *MBO: Blue Collar to Top Executive, An MBO Approach to Long-Range Planning* (also translated into Japanese); *A Strategic Plan for Your Life: A Christian Perspective; Strategic Long-Range Planning;* and *Common Sense Management* — describe personal theories and experiences. He contributed to the books, *Readings in Interpersonal and Organizational Communication* and *International Handbook on MBO.*

The manuscripts, *Production/Operations Management: A Productivity Approach* and *Everybody Wins* are being co-authored. *Tales of Uncle Henry* has been published.

Dr. Migliore produced "Personal Financial Success," an Oral Roberts Ministry video training kit offered on nationwide television, and video/audio tapes to go with his books.

In November 1985, the daily "Managing for Success" cable television program was inaugurated and was on the air until March 1986 on Tulsa Cable. The series began again on Tulsa Cable in September 1986.

In addition, Dr. Migliore is a guest columnist with *The Tulsa Tribune, Tahlequah Pictorial Press,* and contributes a sports feature to the *Jenks Journal.*

Dr. Migliore holds degrees from Eastern Oklahoma State, Oklahoma State University, and St. Louis University, and completed his doctorate at the University of Arkansas. He belongs to the Academy of Management, Planning Executives Institute, and is a senior member of the American Institute of Industrial Engineers.

HIEBERT LIBRARY
3 6877 00006 6638